Understanding Pollution

Oil Spills

Lucy Poddington

First published in 2006 by
Franklin Watts
338 Euston Road
London NW1 3BH

Franklin Watts Australia
Hachette Children's Books
Level 17/207 Kent Street
Sydney NSW 2000

This book is based on *Our Planet in Peril: Oil Spills* by Jillian Powell
© Franklin Watts 2002. It is produced for Franklin Watts by Painted Fish Ltd.
Designer: Rita Storey

Acknowledgements
The publishers would like to thank the following for permission to reproduce
photographs in this book.
Klaus Andrews/Still Pictures: 6; E.J. Bent/Ecoscene: 17b; Randy Brandon/Still Pictures:
4br; Anthony Cooper/Ecoscene: 7b; Digital Vision: front cover, 20c; Fred Dott/Still
Pictures: 4bl; Mark Edwards/Still Pictures: 11cr, 15b, 16b; Natalie Fobes/Corbis: 10b;
Paul Gipe/Still Pictures: 29tr; Greg Glendell/Environmental Images: 25t; Paul Glendell/
Still Pictures: 9t; Al Grillo/Still Pictures: 12tl, 12br; Dominique Halleux/Still Pictures:
11b; John Isaac/Still Pictures: 5c; W. Lawler/ Ecoscene: 13c; McKinnon Films Ltd/
Environmental Images: 27b; McKinnon/ Environmental Images: 10-11t; Chris Martin/
Still Pictures: 23r; Hank Merjenburgh/Environmental Images: 13t, 24t; Sally Morgan/
Ecoscene: 20-21b; NOAA: 14, 15t, 19b, 26c; Jim Olive/Still Pictures: 5t; Christine
Osborne/ Ecoscene: 26b; Edward Parker/Still Pictures: 22b; Popperfoto: 27t; Thomas
Raupach/Still Pictures: 29br; Rockhall/Ecoscene: 18-19; Kevin Schafer/NHPA: 25b; Eric
Schaffer/Ecoscene: 7t; Roland Seitre/Still Pictures: 28-29b; Alex Smailes/ Environmental
Images: 17t; Jean-Marc Teychenne/Environmental Images: 22-23t; Paolo Vaccari/
Environmental Images: 21tr.

A CIP catalogue record for this book
is available from the British Library

ISBN 0 7946 6515 7
Dewey classification: 363.738'2

Printed in Dubai

Contents

Words printed in *italic* are explained in the glossary.

Oil and our world

Oil is a *fuel*. We use it in many different ways in factories, homes, cars and aeroplanes. People drill into the ground and under the sea to find oil. As the oil is carried to where it is needed, it sometimes spills into the sea.

Damage from oil spills

When oil spills into the sea, it harms animals and plants. Many fish, sea birds and *mammals* die. Sometimes oil is washed on to beaches and damages *habitats* on the shore. Oil spills can cause many problems for fishermen and other businesses, too.

People drill under the sea to find oil.

Many sea birds die in oil spills.

4

How do oil spills happen?

Some oil spills happen when people drill for oil. Others happen when the oil is moved around, in tankers or in pipes. If a tanker has an accident, there can be a large oil spill. Sometimes oil is also spilled when the tankers are cleaned.

This oil spill was caused by an explosion on a tanker.

In the 1991 Gulf War, oil was set on fire in Kuwait, a country in the Middle East.

Oil and war

In a war, people may spill oil on purpose, to harm each other. Oil may be set on fire to create black smoke which harms people and animals. The smoke clouds also cause *acid rain* which damages the *environment*.

◆ Problem solving

When there is an oil spill, people need to clean up the oil quickly and carefully. Some people think that there should be a worldwide organisation to clean up oil spills. They say this would be better than each country or organisation working alone.

Why do we need oil?

We use oil in many different ways. It is an important fuel which provides the power for cars, ships and aeroplanes. We also use oil to heat our homes, offices and schools. Oil is needed to make many other things, such as plastic, medicines and paint.

These men are drilling oil from rocks deep under the sea.

What is oil?

Oil is made from the bodies of animals and plants that died millions of years ago. Most oil comes from rocks deep underground or under the sea. When oil comes out of the ground, it is called crude oil. It then goes to an *oil refinery* where it can be turned into petrol or diesel.

Oil is taken from a pipeline on to a tanker at sea.

Road tankers carry petrol from place to place.

Moving oil around

Countries around the world buy and sell oil. Enormous tankers carry the oil across the sea. Oil is also carried in pipelines underground, on special trains and in road tankers. Whenever oil is moved around, spills can happen.

◆ How you can help

If we all use less fuel, oil spills are less likely to happen. Instead of travelling by car, why not try walking or cycling? For longer journeys, go by bus or train. You can also save fuel if you turn down the heating in your home.

About oil spills

Oil spills can happen when there is an accident, such as when a tanker crashes into another ship, or *runs aground* in shallow water. Some oil spills happen when people make mistakes, for example, when tankers or pipelines are not repaired carefully.

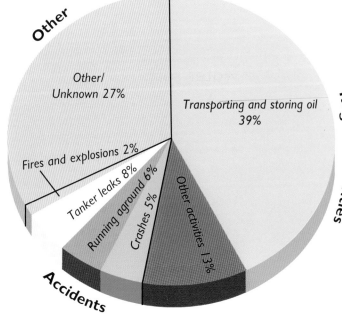

This pie chart shows the different causes of oil spills.

Pie chart labels:
Other
Other/Unknown 27%
Transporting and storing oil 39%
Regular activities
Fires and explosions 2%
Tanker leaks 8%
Running aground 6%
Crashes 5%
Other activities 13%
Accidents

Types of oil
Some oils are light and turn into a *gas* easily. Other oils are heavier. These are harder to clean away when they spill.

Oil slicks
Oil floats because it is lighter than water. When oil spills into the sea, it floats on the surface in a thin layer called an *oil slick*.

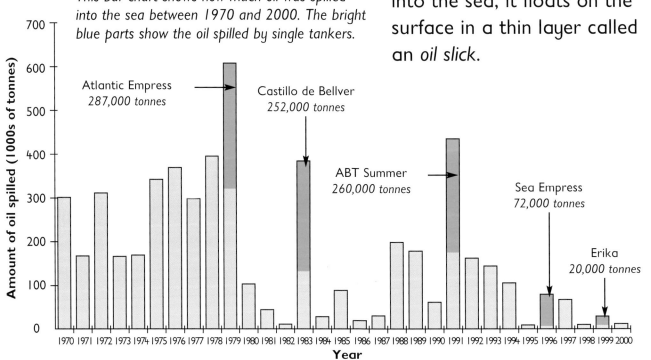

This bar chart shows how much oil was spilled into the sea between 1970 and 2000. The bright blue parts show the oil spilled by single tankers.

Atlantic Empress
287,000 tonnes

Castillo de Bellver
252,000 tonnes

ABT Summer
260,000 tonnes

Sea Empress
72,000 tonnes

Erika
20,000 tonnes

Amount of oil spilled (1000s of tonnes)

Year

Changes taking place

The oil in an oil slick soon starts to change. The lightest part of the oil turns into a gas and mixes with the air. The rest mixes with the sea water to make a sticky liquid that is sometimes called 'chocolate mousse'. If oil mixes with sand on a beach, it may end up on the seabed.

This oil has mixed with the sea water. The mixture looks like chocolate mousse.

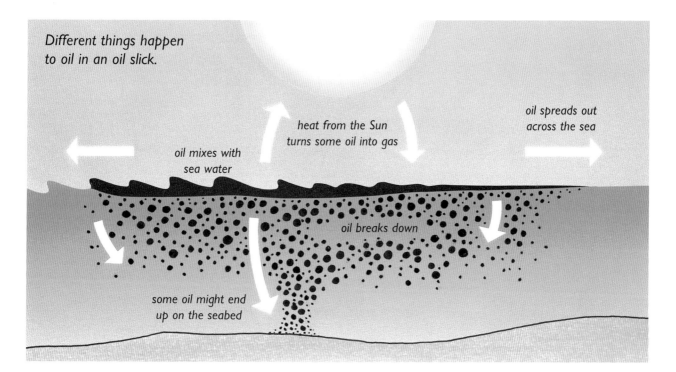

Different things happen to oil in an oil slick.

heat from the Sun turns some oil into gas

oil spreads out across the sea

oil mixes with sea water

oil breaks down

some oil might end up on the seabed

Breaking down

Some oil in the sea breaks down and becomes harmless. Tiny *microbes* in the sea turn the oil into *carbon dioxide* gas and water. This takes a long time to happen.

◆ Science in action

Fill a clear plastic bottle about three-quarters full of tap water. Add some blue food colouring. Then pour in some vegetable oil. Put the top on the bottle and shake it. What happens? Why?

Problems on the shore

When oil spills into the sea near a shore, it causes problems for the people who live there. Fishermen and businesses may lose money. Holiday-makers may stop visiting the place.

Fishing

Oil spills can damage fishing boats and nets. If the oil harms fish, then fishermen may not be able to sell the fish that they catch. Oil spills can also damage *fish farms* near the seashore.

In Saudi Arabia, this oil spill has polluted water used for drinking and washing.

This fish farm has floating barriers to protect it from oil spills.

Water supplies

In some countries, people remove the salt from sea water to make water for drinking and washing. Many power stations and factories also use water from the sea. Oil spills pollute the water so it cannot be used.

Tourism

If oil washes on to a beach, people cannot use the beach for sunbathing and water sports. Tourists may stop visiting the beach, which means that the hotels, shops and other businesses lose money.

Scientists do tests to find out how much damage oil spills cause.

These men are cleaning up oil on a beach in Spain.

◆ How you can help

After an oil spill, charities clean up the beaches and rescue animals and birds. They need money and volunteers to help them do this work.

Wildlife and habitats

People spray water on to beaches to clean up the oil. Spraying water can harm the animals and their habitats.

Oil spills harm all kinds of birds, mammals, fish and plants. Many animals die when their bodies are covered in oil or when they swallow it. The damage is worse if an oil spill happens when birds are looking after their chicks, or fish are laying their eggs. Oil spills can also damage plants which provide food and habitats for animals.

Sea birds

Sea birds find food in seas and oceans. In an oil spill, their feathers get stuck together with oil. This stops them from swimming and flying. When the birds try to clean their feathers, they can swallow oil and die. People rescue birds and clean them with soapy water.

People are cleaning this rescued sea bird.

Mammals

Mammals such as otters and seals have thick fur which helps to keep them warm in the sea. If oil sticks to their fur, they cannot keep warm. Whales and dolphins may also be harmed by oil.

This sea otter was covered with oil. It was taken to a rescue centre and cleaned.

Fish and shellfish

Oil spills may kill fish and stop their eggs from hatching. Other sea creatures, such as prawns, crabs, clams and oysters, also die.

Oil can damage the roots of trees on the shore, like this mangrove tree.

Plants

Oil kills tiny plants in the sea that provide food for fish. Plants on the shore are also damaged. This spoils the habitats where animals live.

◆ Science in action

First find a bird's feather. Then mix up some vegetable oil and cocoa powder in a dish. Add water to the mixture and stir it. Dip the feather into the oil mixture. What happens to the feather? Do you think a bird could fly with feathers like this? Try cleaning the feather with warm water. What happens? Mix some washing-up liquid into the water and try again. How clean is the feather now?

Following oil spills

The wind and waves can make an oil slick move across the sea. When oil spills, scientists study the weather and the way the sea is moving. They also look at maps to try to work out where the oil will go and if wildlife habitats need protecting.

Maps and weather reports help scientists to work out where an oil slick will go.

This scientist is using a map to show where an oil slick is and which way it is moving.

Weather reports

Weather reports give information about which way the wind is blowing and how strong it is. Reports also give warnings of bad weather and storms. This helps scientists to decide which places they need to protect and how to stop the oil from spreading.

In the air

Scientists fly over the sea in helicopters or aeroplanes to see where an oil slick is and how it is moving. It can be difficult to see an oil slick, for example, if it is too dark or foggy. Sometimes seaweed or cloud shadows on the sea can look like an oil slick.

Scientists are going to fly over the sea in this helicopter to look at an oil spill.

Computers show where oil slicks are likely to go.

Using computers

Computers can work out where an oil slick might go and how fast it will move. Scientists type in information and the computer shows what is likely to happen.

◆ **Problem solving**

Scientists are finding new ways to follow oil spills. Some of these methods use *radar* and *lasers*.

15

Cleaning up oil spills

When there is an oil spill, the first thing scientists do is try to stop the oil from spreading. They use barriers to keep the oil away from harbours and wildlife habitats.

Soaking it up

Straw, woodchips and foam soak up oil. They are spread over the oil to act like a giant mop. When all the oil has been soaked up, people in boats collect the mops using nets and rakes.

Booms

A boom is a barrier which stops oil from spreading and moving around the ocean. Booms can float on the sea, or they can act like sponges and soak up oil on the shore.

This boom is made of straw. It will stop oil from coming on to the beach.

Skimmers

Machines called skimmers lift oil from the surface of the sea. Some work like giant vacuum cleaners and suck up the oil. Other skimmers use straw and other materials to soak up the oil.

Skimmers lift oil from the surface of the sea and store it in tanks.

Cleaning the shore

People clean up beaches by shovelling oil into buckets. They also use machines like vacuum cleaners to suck up the oil. Sometimes the oil is washed away with hot water, but this can harm animals and their habitats.

Using hot water to clean beaches can cause extra damage to wildlife.

◆ Science in action

Make your own boom. Take some sand and pile it at one end of a rectangular container to make a beach. Pour water in at the other side of the container. Then make a boom from cotton wool. Place it on the beach near the water. Now pour some cooking oil into the water. Blow it towards the beach. Does your boom keep the oil away from the beach?

Using chemicals

People spray *chemicals* on to oil to break it down and make it less harmful. This must be done carefully. If the chemicals are not used properly, they can cause more damage to animals and habitats.

How chemicals work

Chemicals break down the oil into tiny droplets. These droplets mix with the sea water. Then tiny microbes change the oil droplets into carbon dioxide gas and water, which are harmless. Chemicals do not work on heavy types of oil, or oil that has formed 'chocolate mousse' by mixing with the sea water.

An aeroplane sprays chemicals on to an oil slick.

Chemicals break down oil to make it less harmful.

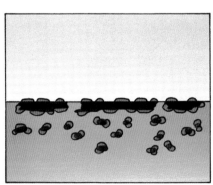

The chemicals stick to tiny droplets of the oil.

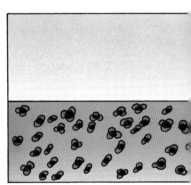

The tiny droplets mix with the sea water.

Spraying chemicals

When there is a small oil spill near the shore, boats are used to spray chemicals on to the oil. Often, small aeroplanes or helicopters are also used to spray chemicals from the air.

Barrels of chemicals are being loaded on to this aeroplane.

Chemicals on the shore

When oil spills on to beaches and shores, scientists check whether it is safe to use chemicals. They find out about the beaches, for example, are they sandy or pebbly? They also find out what type of oil has spilled. Then if it is safe to use chemicals, tractors spray parts of the shore. People spray beaches with chemicals they carry in backpacks.

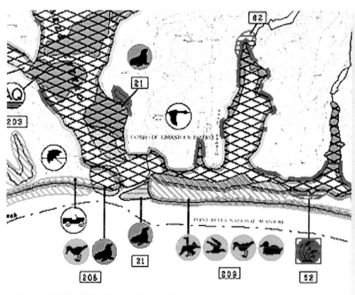

The colours on this map show the different habitats on a shore. The pictures show the animals that live there.

Other clean-up methods

There are different ways of cleaning up oil spills. Before scientists decide which to use, they look at the type of oil spilled, where it is, and what the weather is like. They may need to use more than one method.

Wind and waves can help to break down oil.

Leaving spills alone

If light oil spills, storms and waves may *churn up* the oil and help it to break down. The oil turns into water and carbon dioxide gas. This method works only with light types of oil.

Oil spills damage important habitats such as salt marshes.

Using microbes

Scientists can put tiny microbes into oil to break it down more quickly. The microbes eat the oil and make it less harmful. This method still takes many months and it must be used carefully. It may damage special habitats such as *salt marshes*.

Burning oil spills

Sometimes oil slicks are set on fire, but this causes other problems for the environment. Burning oil gives off clouds of poisonous smoke, so this should not be done near a shore. Sticky waste from the oil may sink to the seabed and harm wildlife.

When oil burns it gives off thick black smoke.

◆ Problem solving

Scientists can grow the microbes that eat oil and break it down. They use these to make new types of chemicals for cleaning up oil spills. New chemicals are also being made which do not harm plants or animals.

Oily waste

When people clean up after an oil spill, they collect oily waste from the sea or from the shore. The oily waste is put into barges or barrels. Then people must get rid of the waste. Different types of waste are dealt with in different ways. The oil may be liquid or solid, or it may have mixed with sand and seaweed.

This dumper truck is clearing oily waste from a beach in France.

Liquid oil from oil spills is taken to an oil refinery.

Liquid oil

Oily waste that is liquid can sometimes be turned into fuel. The waste is taken to an oil refinery, where the oil is separated from any water mixed with it. If the oil and water have formed sticky 'chocolate mousse', it has to be heated or chemicals need to be used to separate the oil from the water.

Oil, sand and seaweed mixture

A mixture of oil, sand and seaweed is poured into a tank or pit. Then machines suck up the oil, leaving the sand and seaweed behind.

A hose sucks up oily waste into a tanker.

Solid waste

Sometimes oil turns into solid lumps called tar balls. If these are small, people can bury them in the sand. Larger tar balls might be burned or buried with other rubbish, or they can be used for building roads.

◆ Problem solving

Helicopters carry *incinerators* to places where oil has spilled. The oily waste is burned in the incinerators.

Large oil spills

Every year there are thousands of oil spills. A large oil spill is when more than 700 tonnes of oil is spilled. In the 1970s there were about 24 large oil spills every year. In the 1990s, the average number of large oil spills each year dropped below ten.

The Exxon Valdez *tanker spilled its oil in Alaska, in the USA.*

Exxon Valdez
24 March 1989

The *Exxon Valdez* tanker ran aground in Alaska and spilled the oil it was carrying. The oil spread across 1,900 kilometres of shoreline. It covered beaches, islands and nature reserves. Thousands of animals and birds died, including fish, otters, bears and eagles.

This bar chart shows the number of large oil spills between 1970 and 2000.

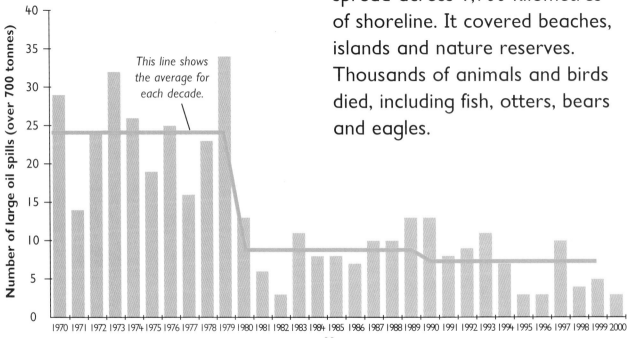

This line shows the average for each decade.

Number of large oil spills (over 700 tonnes)

Year

Braer

5 January 1993
The *Braer* ran aground in the Shetland Islands, off the north coast of Scotland. Stormy weather made it difficult to clean up the oil. However, the waves helped to break down some of the oil.

When oil spilled from the Braer, the rough sea stopped people from cleaning it up.

Sea Empress

15 February 1996
The *Sea Empress* crashed into rocks in south Wales. The oil quickly mixed with the sea water, so chemicals could not clean it up.

◆ **Problem solving**

People are building new tankers which will not spill their oil if there is an accident. The body of these ships has two layers. This means that if the outside layer is damaged, the inside layer will hold in the oil.

Jessica

16 January 2001
The *Jessica* ran aground near the Galapagos Islands, in the Pacific Ocean. These islands are home to many unusual animals and birds. Scientists used booms to stop the oil from spreading, but it reached some beaches and harmed the wildlife.

This kind of cormorant is found only on the Galapagos Islands. These islands have been harmed by oil spills.

The Gulf War

In 1991 there was a war between Iraq and its neighbour, Kuwait. The Iraqi president at the time, Saddam Hussein, ordered his army to spill huge amounts of oil into the Persian Gulf and to set fire to Kuwait's oil wells.

Oil wars

The Gulf War started after Saddam Hussein accused Kuwait of stealing oil from Iraq. Soon afterwards, he sent his army into Kuwait, where the soldiers started to destroy Kuwait's oil supplies.

Giant oil slick

The Iraqi army spilled millions of barrels of oil into the Persian Gulf. This made a huge oil slick which was 50 kilometres long. As the Gulf is a calm sea with land on all sides, the slick did not break up or move away.

During the Gulf War, oil washed on to beaches in the Persian Gulf.

Oil wells in Kuwait gave off clouds of smoke as they burned.

Many birds were killed or injured by oil spills in the Gulf.

Burning oil wells

Kuwait drilled its oil from holes in the ground, called oil wells. When the oil wells were set on fire, they gave off thick black smoke. People became ill when they breathed in the smoke. The smoke also caused acid rain, which damages plants and buildings.

◆ Problem solving

Special ships were used to clean up oil spills after the Gulf War. First, floating booms were put around the oil slicks. Then the ships sucked up the oil, like a vacuum cleaner. The oil was put into large tanks on board the ships and taken away.

Avoiding spills

We cannot stop oil from being moved around because it is an important fuel. But we can make sure that it is carried more safely so that there are fewer spills. We can also improve the ways oil spills are cleaned up.

These coastguards are learning what to do if there is an oil spill.

Rules for oil tankers

People need to follow rules to make sure oil is moved around safely. For example, they must repair oil tankers and pipelines often. Tankers must plan their routes carefully so that they do not crash or go near important wildlife habitats. People can also build new tankers which do not spill oil even if they have an accident.

Special training

People who work on tankers should be trained so that they cause fewer accidents. People also need special training in how to clean up oil spills.

By preventing oil spills, we can help to save sea birds like these pelicans.

Paying for oil spills

It is expensive to clean up oil spills. Those people who cause oil spills should pay for them to be cleaned up. New laws can make sure this happens. This may help to prevent oil spills in future.

Long-term solution

One day the Earth's oil supplies will run out. New ways to make electricity need to be found so that we do not need oil in the future. We can use power from the wind, waves or the Sun.

Wind turbines can be used to make electricity.

◆ How you can help

You can use less oil by choosing electricity that is made by wind or wave power. Some cars run on solar power instead of petrol.

These cars run on electricity which is made using power from the Sun. Cars like this do not need petrol or diesel.

Further information

There are websites where you can find out more about the topics in this book.

http://www.response. restoration.noaa.gov/ kids/kids.html
This website has information on oil spills and ideas for projects and experiments.

http://www.classzone. com/books/earth_ science/terc/navigation/ investigation.cfm
Go to Chapter 7 'What happens when an oil spill occurs?' to find out more about oil spills.

http://news.bbc.co.uk/ cbbcnews/hi/specials
Click on Sea Pollution to find facts, quizzes and competitions.

http://www.mms.gov/ alaska/kids/shorts/ shorts.htm
Find out more about drilling for oil in Alaska.

http://www.darwin foundation.org/misc/ kids/kids.html
Here you can learn about the Galapagos Islands and their animals.

http://www.world wildlife.org/fun/index. cfm
This World Wildlife Fund website has quizzes and games about animals, nature and pollution.

http://www.kidsplanet. org
At the Kids' Planet website, you can learn more about animals and the environment.

Glossary

acid rain
Rain that is more acidic than usual. Acid rain damages plants, wildlife and buildings.

carbon dioxide
A gas which is made up of carbon and oxygen. Carbon dioxide is one of the gases in the air.

chemicals
The Earth and the air are made up of natural chemicals. Other types of chemicals are made by scientists.

churn up
To move around forcefully.

environment
The natural world around us.

fish farms
Places where fish are kept in so they can be fed and looked after.

fuel
Something that gives off heat and energy when it burns.

gas
A substance that is neither a liquid nor a solid. The air is a mixture of gases.

habitats
Places where plants grow or where animals live and find food.

incinerators
Containers for burning rubbish.

laser
A machine that sends out a very strong beam of light.

mammal
An animal whose babies drink milk from their mother's body. Most mammals give birth to live young and have fur.

microbes
Tiny living things, such as bacteria.

oil refinery
A place where oil is separated so that it can be used in different ways.

oil slick
A layer of oil floating on the surface of the sea.

radar
A machine which uses radio signals to find where something is.

run aground
To get stuck on the seabed. Ships can run aground if they go into water that is too shallow.

salt marshes
Wet, grassy places which are often flooded by the sea.

Index